Overwhelmed

How to Stop Trying to Do It All

DEBBIE BARR

AspirePress

Overwhelmed:
How to Stop Trying to Do It All

Copyright © 2024 Deborah Barr
Published by Aspire Press
An imprint of Tyndale House Ministries
Carol Stream, Illinois
www.hendricksonrose.com

ISBN: 978-1-4964-8366-9

The views and opinions expressed in this book are those of the author(s) and do not necessarily express the views of Tyndale House Ministries or Aspire Press, nor is this book intended to be a substitute for mental health treatment or professional counseling. The information in this resource is intended as a guideline for healthy living. Please consult qualified medical, legal, pastoral, and psychological professionals regarding individual concerns. Tyndale House Ministries and Aspire Press are in no way liable for any content, change of content, or activity for the works listed. Citation of a work does not mean endorsement of all its contents or of other works by the same author.

All Scripture quotations, unless otherwise indicated, are taken from the Holy Bible, New International Version,® NIV.® Copyright ©1973, 1978, 1984, 2011 by Biblica, Inc.® Used by permission of Zondervan. All rights reserved worldwide. www.zondervan.com. The "NIV" and "New International Version" are trademarks registered in the United States Patent and Trademark Office by Biblica, Inc.®

Author photo by Melinda Lamm. Cover photo: New Africa/Shutterstock .com. Other images used under license from Shutterstock.com.

Printed in the United States of America
010524VP

Contents

Introduction

Do You Feel Overwhelmed?

Do you sometimes feel that you have too much on your plate and you have no idea how you will get it all done?

Do you feel more driven by what's urgent than by what's really important to you?

When you saw the title of this book, did you identify with the word *overwhelmed*?

If there was even one "yes" among your answers, it may be time to rethink how you really want to live your life.

When we are overwhelmed, stressed-out, and running on empty, it not only robs us of joy; it can also keep us from finding and fulfilling our true purpose in life—"good works, which God prepared in advance for us to do" (Ephesians 2:10).

If your to-do list doesn't reflect your real priorities, and if you're feeling overwhelmed and unfulfilled, you've picked up the right book. In the chapters ahead, you'll find plenty of support and maybe some insights and perspectives you didn't even know you needed. More importantly, you'll learn smart ways to help "overwhelm-proof" your life, both right now and in the future.

If you're ready to move from *overwhelmed* to living life from your sweet spot, this book can help you start the journey!

Chapter 1
I'm So Overwhelmed!

*When I am overwhelmed, you alone
know the way I should turn.*

PSALM 142:3 NLT

AT MEGAN'S WORKPLACE, A DEADLINE IS LOOMING. She wakes up with a bad cold, remembering that starting today, and for the next two weeks, she will be working overtime. She remembers, too, that her boss is unhappy because Megan's reports are overdue.

It's a rainy, windy morning, and on the way to work, Megan's car breaks down. She calls for a tow truck and waits for it on the side of the road. She huddles under a flimsy umbrella that is no match for the pelting rain and tries to ignore her runny nose and pounding headache. She dreads having to call her boss to say she will be late for work. But before she can punch in his number, her cell phone rings. It's her husband, who normally works from home, calling to say he had to leave unexpectedly to see a client in another town.

This means he can't pick up the kids from school today. Megan hangs up, realizing she'll have to find someone to pick up their kids and give them dinner as well because she'll be at the office until at least 8:00 p.m. That thought causes her to suddenly remember that she left *her* dinner—and the permission slip her son needs for today's field trip—on the kitchen counter. She sighs and looks down. That's when she notices that her left shoe is brown and her right shoe is red. It's only 7:30 a.m., but Megan is already overwhelmed.

What Does *Overwhelmed* Mean?

When someone feels overwhelmed, they feel that they have more problems than they can handle. People sometimes compare this overburdened feeling to *bandwidth*—the amount of data an internet connection can handle in a given amount of time. An internet connection with a lot of bandwidth can handle more data faster than an internet connection with lower bandwidth.

In explaining the meaning of *overwhelmed,* bandwidth is a metaphor for how much stress and how many problems we can handle at one time. If someone says, "I don't have the bandwidth for that," they mean they can't handle anything more than they're already dealing with.

We can illustrate the same idea with a hose. A large hose has more "bandwidth" than a small hose because a large hose can carry more water. We can think of a normal amount of emotional and cognitive bandwidth as being like a fire hose that carries more than enough water to put out all the little "fires" that occur in normal daily life, the ones that occur with, say, a typical forty-hour workweek and routine chores like grocery shopping, mowing the lawn, picking your kids up from school, cooking dinner, and walking the dog.

Under normal circumstances, we've got enough bandwidth to keep everything holding steady. All is good. As pressures and problems increase, they require more and more of our emotional and cognitive bandwidth. When we're dealing with many more issues than usual, our bandwidth, as well as our patience, may be strained.

But even that's not necessarily a problem if we're reasonably resilient and the problems are temporary. But when adverse circumstances pile up and up and linger on and on, that *can* be a problem, because now we've got a lot more fires and not enough water to put them all out. When there's no longer even a trickle of water dripping from the hose, our bandwidth has been exceeded. We're now at the point of being overwhelmed.

The word *overwhelmed* can be defined differently, depending on circumstances. It can also mean:

* *Completely covered or submerged*—as when a dam breaks or a river overflows its banks: "The sudden flood of water overwhelmed the valley."

* *Totally defeated*—as in an athletic competition or in war: "The invading army overwhelmed the city."

* *Overpowered, in the sense of too strong*— for example, in cooking: "The extra garlic overwhelmed the sauce."

* *Overcome by a strong emotion or thought*— "The widow was overwhelmed with grief."

What Does the Bible Say?

The word *overwhelmed* appears in the Bible a surprising number of times, and for a surprising number of reasons. The Scriptures are a comforting reality check, reminding us that the human journey has always been a bit overwhelming. Consider these examples of people who were overwhelmed—or spared it—for either positive or negative reasons:

QUEEN OF SHEBA:
Overwhelmed by Abundance

"When the queen of Sheba saw all the wisdom of Solomon and the palace he had built, the food on his table, the seating of his officials, the attending servants in their robes, his cupbearers, and the burnt offerings he made at the temple of the LORD, she was **overwhelmed**." (1 Kings 10:4–6)

ENEMIES:
Overwhelmed in God's Miraculous Rescue

"Remember today that your children were not the ones who saw and experienced the discipline of the LORD your God ... what he did to the Egyptian army, to its horses and chariots, how he **overwhelmed** them with the waters of the Red Sea as they were pursuing you." (Deuteronomy 11:2–4)

DAVID:
Overwhelmed by Guilt

"LORD, do not rebuke me in your anger or discipline me in your wrath. My guilt has **overwhelmed** me like a burden too heavy to bear." (Psalm 38:1, 4)

DAVID:
Rescued from Overwhelming Trouble

"The cords of death entangled me; the torrents of destruction **overwhelmed** me. The cords of the grave coiled around me; the snares of death confronted me. In my distress I called to the LORD; I cried to my God for help ... from a violent man you rescued me." (Psalm 18:4–6, 48)

PAUL:
Forgive to Prevent Overwhelming Sorrow

"You ought to forgive and comfort [that man], so that he will not be **overwhelmed** by excessive sorrow. I urge you, therefore, to reaffirm your love for him." (2 Corinthians 2:7–8)

SOLOMON:
Overwhelmed by Romantic Attraction

"You are as beautiful as Tirzah, my darling, as lovely as Jerusalem, as majestic as troops with banners. Turn your eyes from me; they **overwhelm** me." (Song of Songs 6:4–5)

CROWDS OF PEOPLE:
Overwhelmed by the Presence of Jesus and His Miracles

"As soon as all the people saw Jesus, they were **overwhelmed** with wonder and ran to greet him." (Mark 9:15)

"Some people brought to [Jesus] a man who was deaf and could hardly talk, and they begged Jesus to place his hand on him. After he took him aside, away from the crowd, Jesus put his fingers into the man's ears. Then he spit and touched the man's tongue. He looked up to heaven and with a deep sigh said to him, *'Ephphatha!'* (which means 'Be opened!'). At this, the man's ears were opened, his tongue was loosened and he began to speak plainly.... People were **overwhelmed** with amazement. 'He has done everything well,' they said. 'He even makes the deaf hear and the mute speak.'" (Mark 7:32–37)

Modern Life Can Be Overwhelming

These snapshots of life in biblical times make it clear that feeling overwhelmed is nothing new. For thousands of years, people have sometimes felt overwhelmed when they found themselves in both good and adverse circumstances. Today, we can be just as overwhelmed as they were, and by the same things: material abundance, romantic attraction, danger, guilt, or sorrow. But for us today, there's another factor to consider: the pace and complexity of daily life itself can be overwhelming.

Are people living today more overwhelmed than those who lived in past generations? Many psychologists, counselors, and thoughtful observers of twenty-first century society think so. These experts have described today's experience of being overwhelmed in various ways, but I like this simple definition best: *overwhelmed* is "that state in which there is too much on your plate, and you have no idea how you will ever get it done."[1] And there it is. The reason people are more overwhelmed today than ever before can be explained in just two words: *too much*.

Too Much Information

One day I went to a big-box superstore looking for a specific type of product. I navigated to the correct aisle, where, to my delight, I found an amazing number to choose from. *Wow, just look at all those options!* With some excitement, I started reading labels and comparing prices. I wanted to make a good decision and spend my money wisely.

At first, I felt as if I had found a gold mine. But as I read label after label, considering the merits of each product in light of its price and comparing one product to another, confusion set in. The more I read, the more uncertain I became about which product to choose. I probably stood there reading and comparing and reading and comparing for at least twenty minutes. Then "analysis paralysis" gripped me; I truly could not decide. I was so overwhelmed by all the options that I could not make a choice. I left the store without making a purchase.

> The reason people are more overwhelmed today than ever before can be explained in just two words: *too much.*

I had gone to the store feeling excited and optimistic about the purchase I intended to make. As I walked into the store, I would never have guessed that I would leave empty-handed, disappointed, and discouraged. And as silly as it may sound, I also left feeling a sense of failure. It had been such a simple errand; why couldn't I make a decision?

I now know why. It was because, as a Mayo Clinic article explains, "when there is too much information to process, you may feel cognitive overload. This happens when you reach a point of paralysis of information—not being able to process and then act on what is heard."[2] A Decision Lab article explains this further:

> Since we encounter a vast amount of information, we find it hard to properly sift through it all and prioritize what is important. We might ... find it impossible to make a choice between what product to buy because there are so many options. Being overwhelmed by the options available to us is called the paradox of choice, a phenomenon that suggests that having more options actually makes it harder for us to make decisions.[3]

What happened to me that day in the store was the result of trying to process too much information—what's known as "information overload." The human brain is simply not capable of rapidly prioritizing and processing an avalanche of information. For many of us, information overload goes way beyond choosing products in a store. On the job, we sift through daily emails from colleagues, customers, and management; we take notes in face-to-face meetings and during online meetings or presentations. During the workday we may also need to respond to personal texts from friends and family members. In some jobs, people are expected to absorb a great deal of training information about everything from what to do in an active-shooter situation to the procedure for scheduling vacation time.

One social worker observed that even at home, we are bombarded with an overwhelming amount of information, such as emails from "well-meaning friends sending jokes, stories, and scam warnings, unwanted promos, and a multitude of assorted clutter."[4] At home we also read medication labels, recipes, and nutrition information on food packages, and we sift through our physical mail, separating bills from junk mail (what some now call "land spam"). And then there's the news: on TV, on the radio, online, spoken to us by Alexa, or delivered right to the phone in the palm of our hand.

If you feel that you're dealing with more information than ever before, you're not imagining it. Experts say that we are presented with hundreds or even thousands of pieces of information each day. Consider these astounding statistics from recent years, giving us a snapshot of the amount of information generated on a daily basis:[5]

- Google is searched over 8 billion times.

- 5 billion people use social media platforms.

- 4.75 billion items are shared on Facebook.

- 95 million photos and videos are shared on Instagram.

- 3.7 million new videos are uploaded to YouTube.

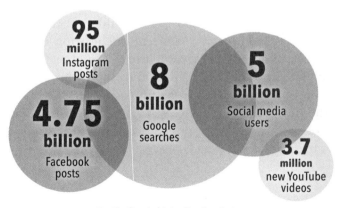

Daily Social Media Statistics

Even several years ago, the information in the world was doubling every few years.[6] This overwhelming flow of information distracts us, interrupts our train of thought, and forces us to choose, sometimes dozens of times a day: should we respond now, save it for later, or ignore it? Each piece of information eats away a tiny chunk of our time and depletes a bit of our finite daily reserves of emotional and mental bandwidth.

Too Much Stuff

In addition to too much information, we also deal with the problem of too much stuff. Let me be quick to say that not everyone in America has too much stuff. Some really don't have enough, not even all of the basics; others have what they need to be comfortable; and some have way, way more than they need. It's fair to say, though, that no matter which category people are in, many—perhaps most—generally want *more* stuff.

That's because in our culture we place a high value on material things. Millions of people are willing to spend more than they earn (that is, to go into debt) in order to get more stuff. They are willing to work to the point of exhaustion, sacrificing time with family and friends, in order to earn more money so they can buy more stuff. In towns and cities across the country, people park their cars on the street because their two-car or three-car garage is full of stuff.

There's nothing inherently wrong with stuff! Nor is there anything inherently wrong with owning stuff. It's just that many possessions come with invisible strings attached. When we have too much stuff that we must insure, keep clean, update, polish, paint, maintain, organize, and/or store, our stuff can become more of a burden than a blessing. In that sense, many things that we own actually own us instead. The time-draining responsibilities that go with owning so much stuff often contribute heavily to our sense of being overwhelmed.

When Joshua Becker and his family "embarked on an intentional journey to own less stuff," they "discovered more money, more time, more energy, more freedom, less stress, and more opportunity to pursue our greatest passions: faith, family, friends."[7] Becker's excitement about the "less is more" lifestyle led him to create a website (becomingminimalist .com) and write a blog and several "declutter your life" books. The theme of his Facebook page is "because the best things in life aren't things."[8] There, page visitors who are drowning in "too much" are challenged by thought-provoking statements such as:

- "We often buy things we don't need, with money we don't have, only to impress people who aren't even watching."

- "Not everything in your past deserves a space in your present."

- "You have to subtract some things from your life to realize just how little they add to it."

- "Owning less means less cleaning, less burden, less anxiety, and less stress each and every day."

Too Much Complexity

The mental, emotional, and physical "hardware" of people today is no different than that of people who lived in past centuries. However, as the opening story illustrates, our more complex lives demand so much more from us than was required from previous generations. Consider two more ways in which the complexity of our lives contributes to our overall sense of overwhelm:

Many Personas

A *persona* is a way of grouping or categorizing people according to their behaviors, interests, or other defining aspects. Companies use customer information such as income, hobbies, and shopping habits to create fictional personas to represent their different types of customers. They might even name the persona something like CEO Harry or Soccer Mom Suzie.

In our personal lives, we may find it necessary to create personas too. Today we have many more kinds of relationship circles than our ancestors had–for example, from high school, college, work, the neighborhood, church, social clubs, the gym, professional groups, and volunteer organizations. We may relate to each group with a different persona. *Psychology Today* writer Dr. Jim Stone explains:

> Most of the people in one circle don't know the people in the other circles.... Facts taken for granted in one circle must be explained in another.... That communication challenge is part of what leads us to develop different personas for interacting in different circles.... The more personas we have, the more disjointed we can feel, and the more work we have to do to keep things straight.... It contributes some of the burden to our overwhelmed minds.[9]

Digital Worries

For most of the time people have been on earth, when one person wanted to speak with another, the only way to do it was face-to-face. Over time, other ways of communicating emerged, and now we have lots of options: letter-writing, telephone, email, chat, social media, video calls, voicemail messages, and texting. Thanks to amazing strides in technology, it's now not only easy to stay in touch with others but also to pay bills, store our documents, and keep an eye on our retirement and credit card accounts, health records, and online orders. That's the upside of living in the digital age.

The downside is that "fingers crossed," always-in-the-back-of-our mind worry that our credit card numbers, tax information, social security number, email address, phone number, and checking, savings, and investment account numbers are all "out there." We hope we have picked strong enough passwords, and we hope those we've trusted with our information have properly protected it. But as we all know, cybercrime and data breaches happen more often than we want to think about. According to a recent Pew Research Center report on data privacy, "In an era where every click, tap or keystroke leaves a digital trail, Americans remain uneasy and uncertain about their personal data and feel they have little control over how it's used."[10] The report found that:

- A majority of Americans are concerned about the privacy of their personal information. Many (71 percent) are especially concerned about how the government uses the data it collects about them, with even more (81 percent) concerned about how companies use their data.

- While some Americans feel confident about managing their online privacy, others (37 percent) feel overwhelmed by the task.

- About one in four Americans (26 percent) say someone has put fraudulent charges on their debit or credit card in the last twelve months.

The same report states, "From social media accounts to mobile banking and streaming services, Americans must keep track of numerous passwords. This can leave many feeling fatigued, resigned and even anxious." The researchers noted that:

- Almost seven out of ten people (69 percent) said they are overwhelmed by the number of passwords they have to keep track of.

- Nearly half (45 percent) feel anxious about whether their passwords are strong and secure.

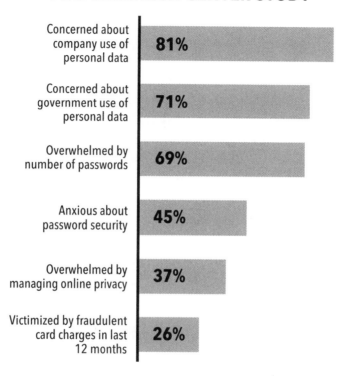

PEW RESEARCH CENTER STUDY

Concerned about company use of personal data	81%
Concerned about government use of personal data	71%
Overwhelmed by number of passwords	69%
Anxious about password security	45%
Overwhelmed by managing online privacy	37%
Victimized by fraudulent card charges in last 12 months	26%

Too Much Bad News

Today's technologies enable rapid news gathering and sharing. This continually directs our attention to the kinds of disasters and traumas that people who lived before us heard about only rarely. Dr. Jim Stone explains more about this phenomenon:

> On the savanna, if something bad happened to one of the members of your tribe, you would hear about it. Most days, though, not much bad happened.
>
> In the modern world there are 7 billion chances for something bad to happen to someone. And our communication systems ensure that, wherever that bad news happens, we will hear about it. A tragedy that might happen once per year in a tribe of 150 will happen many times a minute in a tribe of 7 billion....
>
> While our psychologies are built to process trauma maybe a few times a year, now we have to do so several times per day.[11]

The constant flow of heartbreaking news from all around the world contributes to our sense of being overwhelmed. Of necessity, we have become adept at emotionally sidestepping our way through the newsworthy avalanche of problems: road rage, school shootings, workplace and drive-by shootings, identity theft, addiction, bickering politicians, Medicare fraud, smash-and-grab robberies, assaults on the elderly, riots, corporate greed, and terrorism, among others. In all fifty states, this sad and weighty list of ills is played out in the local news too, which in my city this week included an arrest for infant abuse, a robbery in the Sam's Club parking lot, and a courthouse bathroom assault during a murder trial.

"Too Much" Adds Up to Overwhelming

We can't help but grieve as we see these social evils invading every area of our society. These things weigh heavily on our hearts and increase our concerns about our own personal safety. Nevertheless, we usually push these thoughts to the back of our minds because we must deal with what's more pressing: the pains and problems, bills, potholes, and detours of our everyday lives. We must tend to all the routine things that sustain life for us and our families: grocery shopping; getting gas; housework; mowing the lawn; feeding the dog; dental, doctor, and hair appointments; laundry;

> The constant flow of heartbreaking news from all around the world contributes to our sense of being overwhelmed.

working at our jobs; helping the kids with homework; and so much more. For most of us, *it's a lot*! And most of the time, we manage well enough. But sometimes, when we're weary and our personal cup of problems and tasks is about to overflow, another dose of woe can become for any of us the proverbial "straw that broke the camel's back." We are finally just too tired, too disgusted, and too depleted to think about, much less deal with, even one more thing. We are *overwhelmed*. We have reached the point where our personal combination of problems, fatigue, and must-do's has crossed over the line to "too much." In the words of one writer, this tipping point is the culmination of "many small stressors piling up and making you feel like you cannot endure any additional challenges."[12]

What Happens to Us When We're Overwhelmed?

Here is how two experts have answered this question:

Sociologist Christine Carter, PhD: "When we are busy, busy, busy, it really looks much more like what researchers call cognitive overload.... Cognitive overload is one of those things that hinders our productivity and hinders the power of our mind. It makes it more difficult for us to think clearly and to plan. And it makes it hard for us to control our emotions. It makes it really hard for us to make decisions. It hinders our ability to resist temptations."[13]

Executive Coach Rebecca Zucker: "The cognitive impact of feeling perpetually overwhelmed can range from mental slowness, forgetfulness, confusion, difficulty concentrating or thinking logically, to a racing mind or an impaired ability to problem solve. When we have too many demands on our thinking over an extended period of time, cognitive fatigue can also happen, making us more prone to distractions and our thinking less agile. Any of these effects, alone, can make us less effective and leave us feeling even more overwhelmed."[14]

Sometimes an overwhelming situation resolves in a short amount of time—for example, when a work project is completed. Other times, people may feel overwhelmed by circumstances that don't resolve quickly, such as paying off a major debt.

When a person is chronically overwhelmed, it's often because they are navigating more than one stressful situation at a time, such as grieving the loss of a loved one while dealing with their own or a family member's serious health problem. When a state of overwhelm persists for a long time, or when someone is dealing with multiple simultaneous stressors, it's important to intervene with stress-reducing strategies (more about this in the chapters ahead).

A *Harvard Business Review* article cautions, "When you feel overwhelmed, you may react in ways that not only don't help the situation, but that even make it worse."[15] According to the article, when we feel overwhelmed, we are more prone to make self-sabotaging mistakes. For example:

- We think of things we could do to help ourselves feel less overwhelmed, but we believe we're too busy to act on our ideas. This deepens our sense of being overwhelmed because our inaction makes us feel powerless or incompetent.

- With less cognitive bandwidth available for pondering our options, we may become rigid in our approach to whatever is overwhelming us. This makes us less able to adapt to the situation in ways that would actually be helpful.

- With less emotional bandwidth available for relating to others, we may behave in ways that subtly hold our friends and family at a distance. This is self-sabotaging because when we're overwhelmed, we need emotional support and connection more than usual.

Signs to Watch For

Clearly, being overwhelmed isn't good for us: it erodes our mental health and our relationships. It saps our creativity and leaves us exhausted, unproductive, unhappy, and unfulfilled. Sometimes, however, we don't even realize we are crossing the blurry line between *busy* and *overwhelmed*. To make sure we stay behind that line, we must recognize the signs that let us know we're becoming overwhelmed. These may include:[16]

- Procrastination (purposely delaying dealing with a problem or a project)

- Overreacting to small stresses such as forgetting to charge our phone

- Overeating or drinking too much alcohol

- Irrational thoughts that make problems seem worse and our ability to deal with them seem weaker

- Difficulty falling asleep, or waking up often during the night

- Feeling irritable, anxious, or angry

- Physical discomforts such as headaches, dizziness, feeling tired, fast heartbeat, aches and pains, or digestive issues

- Crying easily

- Feeling paralyzed and unable to function (just as "information overload" rendered me "frozen" and unable to make a purchasing decision on my failed shopping trip)

It's important to maintain a vigilant watch for these signs. They will warn us when we're about to exceed, or may already have exceeded, our mental, emotional, and/or physical capacity to cope.

It's Time to Make a U-Turn

We're living in the most frenetic, stressful, and complex era of human history thus far. And unfortunately, our "too much" society appears to be on track to becoming "way too much." Unless we arm ourselves with new perspectives and new wisdom about how to protect our time and our priorities, we'll likely find ourselves overwhelmed and depleted again and again as the years go by.

The old plan for coping with "too much"—getting up earlier and working harder and longer—only ensures that we'll wind up more overwhelmed than ever. If we're going to find balance, sanity, and a more meaningful life in our "too much" world, we cannot keep doing things in the same old ways. As Joshua Becker phrased the familiar saying on his Facebook page, "If you continue to carry the bricks from your past, you will end up building the same house."

Clearly, it's time to make a U-turn and look for the exit ramp! The great news is that more and more psychologists, lifestyle experts, executive coaches, and others now realize that people need to be equipped with different tools if they are going to "build a different house." The goal of the next two chapters is to help you do exactly that.

We will look at some information about how the human brain works best, offering ideas and tips for working *with* instead of *against* the way we are designed to optimally function. We will also focus on smart strategies for self-managing to prevent (or recover from) being overwhelmed and unproductive. But before we delve into that information, let's pause to focus on five empowering truths that we can totally rely upon whenever life gets overwhelming.

Five Empowering Truths

1. Jesus uniquely understands.

The word *overwhelmed* appears in one other Bible story that was not mentioned in the list at the beginning of the chapter. On the night before Jesus was crucified, Matthew tells us:

> [Jesus] took Peter and the two sons of Zebedee along with him, and he began to be sorrowful and troubled. Then he said to them, "My soul is **overwhelmed** with sorrow to the point of death. Stay here and keep watch with me." Going a little farther, he fell with his face to the ground and prayed, "My Father, if it is possible, may this cup be taken from me. Yet not as I will, but as you will" (Matthew 26:37–39; see also Mark 14:33–35).

More than anyone else we will ever meet, Jesus understands what it is to feel overwhelmed. He experienced the ultimate state of overwhelm when he carried the sins of the entire world to the cross. When we're overwhelmed, he gets us; he has felt what we feel and more. He understands, because on one pivotal night in human history, Jesus was overwhelmed too.

2. *It matters where we focus.*

When David was running for his life, hiding from Saul in a cave, he wrote Psalm 142. Verse three of that psalm is the theme for this chapter: "When I am overwhelmed, you alone know the way I should turn" (Psalm 142:3 NLT). In his deep state of overwhelm, David did not know what to do or which way to turn. This can also be true of us when we are overwhelmed. David realized that even though he didn't know what to do, God alone *did* know what he should do. And this, too, is true for us always.

When we are overwhelmed, God alone knows what we should do. That's why we must keep our focus more on God than on the circumstances that are overwhelming us. In other words, instead of gazing in desperation at the problem, and occasionally glancing toward God, we should do the reverse: we should fix a trusting gaze intently upon God, just as David did when his life was in jeopardy. And while we must attend to our problems, our worry should be, by comparison, like a glance.

The bottom line is this: when we feel overwhelmed, it matters where we focus. When problems threaten to overwhelm and undo us, David's counsel, from his own experience, is: "Look to the LORD and his strength; seek his face always" (1 Chronicles 16:11).

3. God's truths are immutable.

One amazing fact about God is that he is immutable. *Immutable* means *not capable of change*. Because God is immutable, so are his promises. Dr. Charles Stanley wrote, "God's truth does not change from year to year or decade to decade or century to century. It does not vary depending on current style or ... popular opinion. In a world of constant change, his truth remains constant."[17] When we are overwhelmed, we can find great comfort and flawless counsel in the Bible, God's great treasury of immutable truth.

4. God's got our back.

No matter how overwhelmed we may be, no matter what burden we're carrying or what we're facing, there's no need to panic; God's got our back. If we look to him and place our trust in him, he will carry us through our most overwhelming challenges, sometimes in ways we would never expect. As Dr. David Jeremiah has written, "God will give you overcoming strength for overwhelming moments."[18]

5. Be overwhelmed—in a good way.

When we are overwhelmed, stressed out, and emotionally frayed, we can easily lose sight of the real purpose of our lives. That purpose, first stated so beautifully in the 1600s as part of the Westminster Confession of Faith, "is to glorify God and to enjoy him forever."[19] Thus, we're actually *meant* to be overwhelmed—in a good way and in the best possible sense of the word—not by what's toxic or taxing, but by the beauty and majesty of God himself.

Overwhelmed is the title of a beautiful song by the band Big Daddy Weave. The message of the song is, *Be overwhelmed. Be overwhelmed by the majesty of God, his creation, his beauty, and all that he is.* The lyrics celebrate the wonder and glory of God. They tell us that we can unashamedly worship him and delight in him because he regards us with such mercy.

When we're overwhelmed in this good way, we've returned to our purpose, our spiritual "sweet spot." In this context, we have a greater desire to live as God intended, using our gifts and talents to do meaningful work that we enjoy and which also brings glory to God. Are you enjoying God? Do your life and work glorify (honor and call attention to) God? If you're not living out your purpose, not enjoying your job, not enjoying God, and you don't feel that you are doing the work you were designed to do ... the next two chapters will help!

Chapter 2
Jars of Clay

Beware the barrenness of a busy life.
ATTRIBUTED TO SOCRATES

WHEN THE APOSTLE PAUL DESCRIBED THE relationship between believers and God's Spirit within us, he referred to the Spirit as "this treasure" and to us as "jars of clay" (2 Corinthians 4:7). His point was that compared to the infinite, all-surpassing power of God, we mortal "jars" are fragile and frail, severely limited by the constraints of our humanity.

Paul was right, of course. We only have so much time on this earth, and unlike God, we have limited stores of mental, physical, and emotional energy. In the crunch and crush of daily life, it's not that hard to overwhelm a fragile jar of clay. In Barbara Reich's book *Secrets of an Organized Mom*, she tells readers,

> When we're looking at the master calendar or sitting down at the computer to answer email or pay bills, life can start to feel ... overwhelming. So many things *must* get done, and so many other things *should* get done. As a result, the things that we'd love to do can get shoved way down to the bottom of the to-do list. If there is one message you should take away ... it's that you can't do it all.[20]

Few people would disagree. At some level we all know that we can't do it all. But that doesn't stop us from trying! Because "so many things *must* get done," we sometimes push ourselves across the line to "too much." When we do, hopefully we will quickly recognize the symptoms of being overwhelmed—exhaustion, irritability, tearfulness, headaches, etc. If we are wise, we will heed what these signs are telling us to do: slow down, take a break, get some rest, and maybe figure out how to do some things differently.

But if we ignore the signs and force ourselves to keep pushing past our God-given limits, sooner or later there will be a price to pay. And it's never worth what it will cost us. If we are chronically overwhelmed and find ourselves crossing the line to "too much" again and again, it's time to reassess what we're doing—and whether we really want to go where living overwhelmed will inevitably take us.

What Were You Born to Do?

While none of us has the time or superhuman energy to do everything we would like to, we *do* have the time and energy for everything that really matters. That is, if we are willing, we will be given everything we need to accomplish what God has preplanned for us in this life. Our assurance of this is Ephesians 2:10: "We are God's handiwork, created in Christ Jesus to do good works, which God *prepared in advance* for us to do."

Concerning this amazing verse, John Vaughan, who preached in the early twentieth century, taught:

> You may be quite sure that any "work" which God hath "prepared" for you, will have a particular adaptation to your character, to your position, and to your strength. God never gives His work indiscriminately. To each his own. His "works" are not suited to everybody alike. You could not do mine; and I cannot do yours.... In the fact that the "work"—whatever it be—is God's own appointment for you, there is a sure warrant of success. He planned and constructed it before you touched it.[21]

Theologian Henry Alford explained Ephesians 2:10 like this:

> We might say of the trees, they were created for fruits which God before prepared that they should bear ... [he] defined and assigned to each tree its own [fruit], in form, and flavour, and time of bearing. So in the course of God's providence, our good works are marked out for and assigned to each one of us.[22]

Each of us is absolutely unique. According to the National Forensic Science Technology Center, "no two people have ever been found to have the same fingerprints—including identical twins." Identical twins also have slight differences in their DNA.[23] No two people who have ever lived have had the same combination of physical traits, natural talents, spiritual gifts, personality, and intellect.

God's plan for each person's life is as unique as they are, with unique opportunities "to do good works, which God prepared in advance for us to do." To say that another way, in God's plan, every person has a unique purpose. That purpose is consistent with our personalities, natural strengths and talents, spiritual gifts, and heart's desires. As we explore these four aspects of our own lives, we begin to discover our true purpose—what we were designed by God to do.

Personality

Are you introverted, extroverted, or a little of both (an ambivert)? Do you make decisions based more on fact and logic or on feelings and intuition? Are you spontaneous or are you a planner? Personality tests can make you aware of your "default settings" and point you toward paths that align with how you're wired. They can also be fun to take and then discuss with those who know you well. There are self-assessment tests to measure everything from perfectionism and emotional intelligence to career aptitude and "driving personality." Many are available for free online. Or if you prefer, a professional counselor or psychologist can administer "old school" personality tests such as the Myers-Briggs or DiSC and discuss the results with you in an office setting.

Natural Strengths and Talents

According to the Gallup organization, most of us spend our lives trying to fix our weaknesses when we should instead be developing our natural strengths and talents. It makes more sense to focus on these, Gallup experts say, because we have a limited amount of time to invest in ourselves. So, some thoughtful self-observation is in order:

- What do others affirm that you do well?

- What do you easily succeed at doing?

- How can you make what's naturally strong even stronger?

In the book *Now, Discover Your Strengths*, the Gallup organization explains that you can identify your natural strengths and talents by paying attention to the following four clues.[24]

🔍 CLUE 1: *Response under Stress*

Your spontaneous reactions in times of stress are clues to your natural talents. Do you take charge? Find the humor in the situation? Respond with empathy? Calmly analyze what's happening? Stress brings to the surface inborn patterns that hint at your underlying strengths and talents.

🔍 CLUE 2: *Yearnings*

If you yearn for something, especially early in life, it reveals the presence of a talent. Yearnings are the "specialties" your brain naturally urges you toward. The *Strengths* book explains, "Your yearnings reflect the physical reality that some of your mental connections are simply stronger than others." It offers these examples:

> At thirteen Picasso was already enrolled in adult art school. At five the architect Frank Gehry made intricate models on the living room floor with wood scraps from his father's hardware store. And Mozart had written his first symphony by the time he turned twelve.

I can add my own story here. When I was in first grade, I carefully copied the words of my beginner's reading primer and proudly announced to my family that I had "written a book." (I didn't know about plagiarism yet!) Here I am, all these years later, writing my tenth book, the one you're reading. Again, some thoughtful self-analysis is in order:

- What did you yearn for when you were very young?

- What do you yearn for now?

CLUE 3: *Rapid Learning*

The ability to rapidly learn a new skill indicates the presence of an inborn talent. The *Strengths* book advises that no matter what skills you have learned quickly, you should look deeper for the talents behind them.

CLUE 4: *Satisfaction*

If doing a certain activity gives you a feeling of satisfaction, it's probably because you're tapping into a natural strength or talent while doing it. The explanation is again found in what's happening in the brain: "Your strongest synaptic connections are designed so that when you use them, it feels good."

Spiritual Gifts

Your spiritual gifts are a strong indicator of the kinds of "good works" God has planned for you to do. It makes sense that he would gift you in ways that fit his plans for you. Every Christ follower has at least one, and often more than one, spiritual gift. Spiritual gifts are mentioned in three places in the New Testament:

- Romans 12:6–8

- 1 Corinthians 12:4–11, 28–30

- Ephesians 4:11–13

In all, eighteen different gifts are named. These gifts, given to every believer by the Holy Spirit, fall into four basic categories:

1. Serving
2. Teaching
3. Worshiping
4. Witnessing

If you're not sure what your spiritual gifts are, the Resources section at the end of this book provides links to two online assessment tools that can help you discover your spiritual gifts.

Desires of Your Heart

There's one more thing to consider, especially when you're overwhelmed in your present circumstances and wondering if God has a different path in mind for you. It's found in Psalm 37:4, which promises, "Take delight in the LORD, and he will give you the desires of your heart." What does your heart desire? Matthew Henry reflected on this verse in his commentary:

> We must make God our heart's delight and then we shall have our heart's desire.... This pleasant duty of delighting in God has a promise annexed to it, which is very full and precious, enough to recompense the hardest services: *He shall give thee the desires of thy heart.* He has not promised to gratify all the appetites of the body and the humours of the fancy, but to grant all the desires of the heart, all the cravings of the renewed sanctified soul. What is the desire of the heart of a good man? It is this, to know, and love, and live to God, to please him and to be pleased in him.[25]

The more you delight in the Lord, the more he delights in fulfilling your heart's desires! You don't have to hold back—you can pour out to the Lord the deepest desires of your heart. What brings you joy? What makes you "light up"? What do you want most? What are your most cherished dreams for your life?

The deepest desires of your heart are huge indicators of the kinds of "good works" you are meant to do. Those desires, along with your God-given personality, inborn strengths and talents, and spiritual gifts are the clues that point you to the "sweet spot" of your true purpose.

The Sweet Spot

Speaking to a conference audience, sociologist Christine Carter delivered a message she called "Full Plate, Empty Life." She told them, "The wonderful thing is that we all have a sweet spot.... We just need to get out of our own way in order to find it." Dr. Carter ended her presentation with a variation of the quote from Socrates that opens this chapter: "Beware the banality of a busy life." Then she said, "To that I would add: behold the astonishing richness that comes when we live life from our sweet spot."[26]

Many people embark on a lifelong quest to find their sweet spot. Those who are fortunate to find it live it to the fullest when they sync their lives with the one who created them. When we are enjoying God, using the attributes he has woven into our being and immersed in the work he prepared for us in advance, our cup is truly full. We're in our ultimate sweet spot, doing what we were born to do. That's where the truest "astonishing richness" Christine Carter spoke of is fully experienced. But because life can be so utterly overwhelming, "getting out of our own way" is often our hardest struggle. Many of us can clearly envision our sweet spot, and though we long for it, we don't know how to maneuver our circumstances so we can step into it. How do we begin?

Establishing Priorities

Establishing priorities is the first step toward "getting out of our own way." Priorities can help us chart a course to the things our hearts say matter most. In his book *Forward*, Dr. David Jeremiah writes,

> You only have one life on earth. Since time doesn't move backward, you have a certain allocation of hours, days, or years left to you. Every one of them from this split second onward is the future. There's no time to waste. You want to live every day without reservation, without retreating from the cause, and with no regrets when you're finished.[27]

To live like that, we must have clearly defined priorities. Priorities govern what we'll say yes to, what we'll say no to, and how we will manage our time. If we're chronically overwhelmed, setting priorities will help bring order to our chaos. Author Charles Hummel said, "The first step to regain control of time is to decide what activities are most important so that we can plan to give them proper priority."[28]

Each person's matrix of responsibilities, relationships, desires, obligations, and practicalities is as unique as their fingerprints. That's why no one else can determine our priorities for us. Only we know what matters the most to us. How we choose our priorities and manage the details of each one is something we customize and then continually adjust as our circumstances change. It's helpful to first decide on our main governing priorities, such as, for example, God, others, self, and "everything else"—work, hobbies, home maintenance, and whatever remains that requires our time and energy. Even with just those four broad priority categories, there's quite a bit to consider. Here's some food for thought about each one:

God

Making God our highest priority makes sense in light of two Bible verses, one from the Old Testament and one from the New Testament. God himself gave us the command, "You shall have no other gods before me" (Deuteronomy 5:7). If that leaves any doubt as to the priority God should have in our lives, the words of Jesus clarify it: "Seek first his kingdom and his righteousness" (Matthew 6:33).

It's important to consider what "God as highest priority" means in terms of time and money. Allotting daily time to read the Bible? Attending church or a study group? Using our talents in a faith-based context, such as volunteering at church? Does it mean adding a new category in the family budget for giving?

Other People

Relationships are "expensive" when it comes to the time and effort it takes to sustain them. According to psychologist Robin Dunbar, we can only handle a total of about 150 meaningful relationships at a time, including just five close relationships.[29] Dunbar likes to represent these friend connections as a series of circles within circles. The innermost circle represents our romantic relationship. After that, the "circles of friendship" stack like this, with each circle including the number of people in the circle before it:

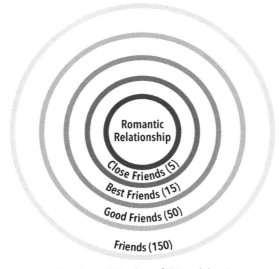

Dunbar's "Circles of Friendship"

In an interview with *The Atlantic* magazine, Dunbar explained that layers of friendship exist because we have a finite amount of time to invest in relationships with others. He noted that introverts prefer to have fewer friends so they can spend more time with each person. Extroverts want more friends and prefer to invest less time in each relationship. Those with very large families have fewer friends because they prioritize relationships with their family members.

Dunbar told the *Atlantic* interviewer that it takes an investment of about two hundred hours of time over a period of a few months to "move a stranger into being a good friend." So because friendships are expensive in terms of time, and our capacity for close relationships is limited, it's important to choose our priority people carefully.

The wonderful thing to keep in mind is that—unlike money, job titles, fame, and material possessions—people are eternal. The time we invest in our relationships with friends and family members can literally have an eternal impact.

Self

In Matthew 22:39, Jesus gives us a command: "Love your neighbor as yourself." The "love your neighbor" part is pretty clear. But what about the "as yourself" part? Blogger Doug Bender writes,

> Following Jesus means you put yourself second [to God and others]. But that does not mean you stop taking care of yourself. Quite the opposite! If you live your life saying, "I am second," then you will also need to say, "I have to do this for me." The most generous people know how to care for themselves. If you don't, you will experience burnout.[30]

In *A Season at Home,* a book for stay-at-home moms, I wrote about the experience that changed my thinking about what it means to be selfish. I was flying from North Carolina to Los Angeles with my two-year-old son. I had heard the preflight safety speech many times before, but on this trip, maybe because my toddler was with me, I paid more attention. The flight attendant explained that if cabin pressure was lost, oxygen masks would drop in front of us from above. She said, "If you are traveling with a small child, put your own oxygen mask on before attempting to assist the child." That bothered me. If my son and I both needed oxygen, wouldn't it be awfully selfish to take care of myself first?

It took a little while for me to realize that the flight attendant's instructions were actually wise. What if a child resisted their parent's attempt to put the mask on them? Then what if the parent passed out from lack of oxygen while trying to win the power struggle? Without the parent's help, the child might then pass out too. By instructing the parent to do the "selfish" thing, the airline ensured a much greater chance that both parent and child would get oxygen.

> When we are overwhelmed, we can't be emotionally present, productive, or of much help to others.

In the book I wrote, "The lesson I learned that day is this: it's not selfish for mothers to get their own needs met; it's smart." In two subsequent books for caregivers, I passed this same lesson along, urging caregivers to prioritize their own self-care *so that* they can take good care of the other person.

Caring for ourselves is an appropriate expression of self-love that enables us to love others. Whether we are a parent, spouse, employee, or friend, when our own cup is empty and we are overwhelmed and irritable, we can't be emotionally present, productive, or of much help to others. Bender agrees:

> If you do not sleep, eat or take care of your physical needs, then you will find yourself with a short temper and a cranky personality.... Even if you wish you could give, give, give and go, go, go, God made you to be a finite being with limits. Recognize those limits and you will be happier and better positioned for generosity.[31]

The obvious conclusion is that if we are to really fulfill the command to love our neighbor, our own "cup" must first be filled. That may mean designating self as a "priority person" in our own schedule. For example, we all need down time. It's okay, and often quite necessary, to plan ahead for personal downtime by blocking it out in our schedule. Leadership coach Scott Monty writes,

> Remember that busyness can mask priorities. Take the time you need for an ordered mind and a calm, rational approach to your week. And take time to reflect on what matters most to you. It could be family, work, goals, a project you're working on—whatever. But if you're mired in distractions, frivolous activity, or things that

are keeping you from concentrating on what matters, perhaps it's time to step away. Put down the phone. Turn off the notifications. Shut the laptop. There's meaning in self-reflection and time alone. Go just be with yourself for a bit. Less dot com. More dot calm. Enjoy the quiet.[32]

Everything Else

This "potpourri" category has many subcategories, such as job, further education, chores, hobbies, and many other things. These subcategories often have the greatest potential for overwhelming us, so this is where the most pruning may be required. Can we work forty hours a week, coach our child's team, keep the lawn mowed, lead a Bible study, participate in a neighborhood book club, volunteer at the food bank, spend quality time with our family, and still have some personal downtime? As has been noted, no one can do it all. Each person must decide what commitments are realistic and a worthy investment of their time.

It can be hard, even painful, to scale back to a few manageable priorities, but that's one of the secrets to avoiding an overwhelmed life. We must each decide what matters, what doesn't matter, and what matters but belongs in another season of our life or on another person's plate. Then, with our priorities clearly in mind, it's important—*really important*—to make sure that our schedule continually reflects the priorities we have chosen.

Protecting Priorities

Here are three keys that can help us protect our priorities and keep us from becoming overwhelmed.

 KEY 1: Narrow the Channel to Strengthen the Stream

When I attended my first writer's conference many years ago, I never expected to learn a writing tip that would become a guiding principle for my life. The seminar teacher told us aspiring writers that if we wanted to be successful at our craft, we would have to "narrow the channel to strengthen the stream." More than anything else I learned at that conference, that pearl of wisdom has stuck with me through the years.

The teacher explained that just as water flows more powerfully through a narrow channel than through a broad one, writers must direct their time and energy into the "narrow channel" of writing instead of spreading them across multiple pursuits that would take time away from writing. In order to fully say yes to writing, we would sometimes have to say no to good, interesting, and enjoyable things.

It was a reality check I needed to hear. I got the message: To succeed, we would have to invest our time, talent, and finite supply of mental and physical energy as wisely as possible. In time, I came to realize that this excellent advice was not just for writing, but for every area of life. What I learned from my writing teacher boils down to two key life lessons:

1. Because life is too short to do everything, we must choose priorities.

2. Then we must "narrow the channel" so we can actually live by the priorities we have set.

🔑 KEY 2: Resist the Tyranny of the Urgent

"Your greatest danger is letting the urgent things crowd out the important." Those words from a factory manager were life-changing for Charles Hummel. In his iconic book, *The Tyranny of the Urgent*, he wrote, "[The factory manager] didn't realize how hard his advice hit. It has often returned to rebuke me by raising the critical problem of priorities."[33]

If we have thoughtfully considered the attributes that God has uniquely woven into us and honed our priorities accordingly, we know what's important, what it takes to live in our "sweet spot." But as Hummel pointed out, "We live in constant tension between the urgent and the important." The phone never stops ringing, the emails never end, and distractions abound. The danger is that if we keep responding to the unplanned things that are urgent, or appear to be, we may never get around to the things that are actually much more important and in sync with God's purposes for our lives. Hummel is famous for pointing out that every need, no matter how urgent, is not necessarily a call for us to meet it:

> The call must come from the Lord who knows our limitations.... It is not God who loads us until we bend or break with an ulcer, heart attack or stroke. These largely come from our inner compulsions under the pressure of external demands.[34]

Prayer helps us to discern what we should agree to do and what we should pass on. We keep our priorities on track, not by impulsively leaping at every opportunity or automatically heeding every demand (lest we disappoint someone), but by asking, "Lord, what would you have me do?" If we make it our practice to not decide immediately, but allow time for reflection, we may return a different answer than if we had responded right away.

 ### KEY 3: Set Boundaries

Another way to safeguard our priorities is by setting appropriate boundaries. Boundaries can be physical and tangible, or they can be intangible. Our skin is a tangible boundary that defines what is "us" and what is "not us." Our skin boundary also protects us by keeping germs out of our body and keeping our blood, bones, and everything else inside. A fence is a tangible boundary that defines the yard we are responsible for and separates it from the yard next door that we are not responsible for.

For our purposes, the best example of an intangible boundary is the word *no.* Sometimes we're overwhelmed because we're overcommitted, and we're overcommitted because we just can't bring ourselves to say no. It's a common problem. Organizational expert Barbara Reich realized this when she began to work with a client who sought her help in getting organized. "I realized that the problem wasn't so much that she was disorganized; it was that she said yes to every invitation or request for her time. My first task with the overscheduled moms I work with is to teach them now to say no."[35]

When we find ourselves overwhelmed by tasks that aren't even on our priority list, it's often because we've said yes when we should have said no. Why do we do that? Reasons vary, but some people may find it hard to say no if they:

- Lack clarity about their priorities, or are not solidly committed to them

- Want the approval of others

- Yield to pressure from people who want them to volunteer, work overtime, or attend social functions

When we say no, we are stating our boundary: This is what we will do or won't do; this is what we will allow or won't allow. We never need to feel guilty about saying no to things that conflict with our priorities. When we say no to a nonpriority, it allows us to say yes to what's more important to us.

For example, if we have arranged our schedule so we can have a regular date night with our spouse or attend our child's sports events, we don't have to think twice about saying no to grabbing dinner after work with a colleague if it conflicts with our more important priority of spending time with our family. *No* is a protective boundary that we must use, always kindly and graciously of course, to decline anything we don't want to do or don't have time to do.

Make a U-Turn Slowly

In *The Tyranny of the Urgent*, Charles Hummel wisely cautioned his readers, "Don't try to reorganize your life on paper and then hope to live a new schedule immediately."[36] If we have lived with undefined priorities or have done things a certain way for many years, it's hard to just throw old habits into reverse.

As what is really important to us comes into sharper focus and we realize that our priorities must shift, the best approach is to implement just one or two changes at a time. While making changes may seem a bit daunting, there are many smart strategies that can help us as we journey toward our sweet spot. That's the focus of the next chapter.

Chapter 3
Herding Cats

*Dogs come when they're called. Cats take
a message and get back to you later.*

ELOISA JAMES

IF YOU HAVE A CAT, OR ARE NEIGHBOR TO ONE, YOU
know that cats are notoriously independent creatures.
They hunt alone and they don't live in groups. When
they live with us, they don't play "fetch" or jump
up and down when we come home. It has also been
humorously noted that cats "do not have owners; they
have caretakers whom they allow to live with them."[37]

Needless to say, cats are not amenable to herding. If
we say that something is "like herding cats," we're

saying that it is a very difficult, if not impossible, thing to do. When we are overwhelmed, trying to get a grip on all the out-of-control parts and pieces of our lives can feel like "herding cats." And while cat herding is futile, it's actually possible to *manage* our "cats"—our burdensome challenges and stressors—in ways that can make life less overwhelming.

Your Brain on Overwhelm

Our natural response to feeling overwhelmed is to double down—getting up earlier and earlier and working harder and longer. We become zealous multitaskers, doing several things at once to quickly accomplish as much as possible. Multitasking makes us feel like we're making the best use of our time and getting more done. The truth, however, is that we're as good at multitasking as we are at herding cats. Multitasking is a myth.

How Multitasking Affects the Brain

Neuroscience has revealed a disappointing reality: multitasking does not work. In fact, it *cannot* work. According to researchers, "The human mind and brain lack the architecture to perform two or more tasks simultaneously."[38] In other words, the human brain is capable of focusing on only one thing at a time. When people think they are multitasking, what they are really doing is task switching. Task switching means rapidly turning one's attention from one thing to another again and again. Multitaskers are actually just good at task switching. And the problem with task switching, aka multitasking, is that it is terribly inefficient.

Multitasking slows us down because every time the brain leaves one topic unfinished to move on to another, it must reorient itself to the new topic. This slows our thinking, researchers explain, "because we have to bring back to mind the new task's representation and then use it to allocate attention to information that is relevant to perform the new task."[39] While some people insist that multitasking is a time saver, it's really not; it actually adds time. What's worse is that when we rapidly task switch, according to the Dana Foundation, "valuable information, without fail, falls through the cracks."[40]

So now we know the truth: the "task switch costs" of multitasking make it slower than was once believed, and also inevitably lead to mistakes. In addition, multitasking depletes the brain's supply of glucose, its main fuel. This can lead to brain fatigue, which makes it harder to stay focused, harder to be productive, and harder to remember things.[41]

According to the Dana Foundation, "Studies consistently show that human beings are terrible multitaskers." Psychologist Jade Wu agrees: "Multitasking works about as well as texting while driving—which is to say, it doesn't."[42] Thus, multitasking no longer draws the applause it once did, especially from the business world. Science is now pointing us all to what does actually work, which is *monotasking*.

The Brain and Monotasking

Whether we call it monotasking, single tasking, or unit tasking, it is now clear that our brains are "wired" to focus on just one task at a time. Single tasking is better than rapid task switching, no matter what we're trying to accomplish. It enhances our performance whether we are working in an office, shopping online, or cleaning up at home, and it keeps us safer when we're navigating bumper-to-bumper traffic on the freeway. Neuropsychologist Cynthia Kubu affirms that "we unequivocally perform best one thing at a time."[43] Other experts advocate monotasking as well:

- Julia Martins, a writer for the workplace productivity company Asana, endorses monotasking because it "allows you to align your attention with your intention for the day and focus on one task at a time."[44]

- In her "Full Plate, Empty Life" lecture, Dr. Christine Carter told her audience, "We can move from the idea that multitasking and busyness is a sign of our productivity ... to the truth, which is that we're actually more productive when we single task.... Our brains are not computers. They were not designed to run multiple apps at any one given time."[45]

- Cognitive neuroscientist Dr. Sahar Yousef likens the time and energy lost in multitasking to a tax. "It's almost always more efficient to monotask," she says. "Focus on one thing and move on when you're done, so you don't pay unnecessary switching taxes."[46]

It's been said that there is an exception to everything, and this is true of multitasking. While 98 percent of human beings cannot multitask, about 2 percent of people are "supertaskers" who actually can. Their brain structure is different from the brain structure the rest of us have. If you're one of the rare supertaskers, enjoy your superpower! Otherwise, *Psychology Today* writer Garth Sundem advises, "if you're not a supertasker, the overwhelming message of science is this: just give it up already! By multitasking, you do everything less well. Instead, if you want to get the most done right, design your life to monotask. Your brain will thank you for it."[47]

MULTITASKING STATISTICS

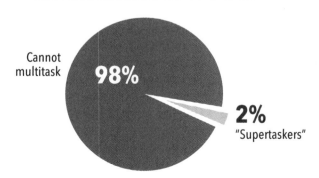

Cannot multitask **98%**

2% "Supertaskers"

The Brain and Fight-or-Flight

When we feel overwhelmed, whether our instinct is to multitask or not, we may react in another way that is puzzling, even to us. Why, in the words of psychologist Jade Wu, do we sometimes sit "mindlessly clicking a retractable pen for minutes at a time" when we are overwhelmed?[48] Why, when we have so much on our plate, do we spend time randomly scrolling through social media? Or why, with to-do list in hand, do we binge-watch TV reruns? It's because, Wu says, when we're overwhelmed, the brain doesn't see a to-do list; it sees a threat:

> *I might not be able to meet the deadline!*
>
> *I might fail!*
>
> *I might disappoint someone!*
>
> *Maybe I'm not doing enough!*

When the brain perceives a threat, it automatically launches into fight-or-flight" mode, triggering the stress hormones cortisol and adrenalin. This is a survival mechanism that enables us to either fight against what's threatening us or run away from it in time to save our life. In prehistoric times, the fight-or-flight reaction could have kept us off a wild beast's dinner menu.

Today, it's an overreaction to many of the non-threats we face, including the feeling of being overwhelmed. Fight-or-flight kicks in because our brain doesn't distinguish between a threat that's life-threatening and one that isn't. Because the brain doesn't know that missing a work deadline won't kill us, it goes into fight-or-flight mode to protect us.

Sometimes, however, instead of fighting or fleeing, we just freeze. And according to Dr. Wu, feeling overwhelmed causes us to "land somewhere between freeze and flight, which shows up as procrastination." When we're mindlessly pen-clicking, scrolling through social media posts, or binge-watching reruns, we are procrastinating. This "freeze" allows us to temporarily avoid the tasks that are overwhelming us.

Overwhelmed on the Inside

When we procrastinate because we're overwhelmed, it's a sign that we need to explore ways to remedy our stressful circumstances. However, procrastination isn't always due to pressures that are external to us. Sometimes we procrastinate because of something on the inside of us that needs our attention. If you tend to procrastinate, and if one of the following reasons applies to you, give thoughtful attention to what your procrastination may be trying to tell you.

Procrastination and the Desire for Meaningful Work

One workplace-productivity writer observed, "Without insight into why your work matters, it's hard to motivate yourself to get that work done."[49] Whether we work for a paycheck or on a volunteer basis, if what we're doing is not meaningful to us or if we do not enjoy it, we may struggle to keep doing it. That inner struggle for meaning may show up as procrastination.

- Is your paid or volunteer work meaningful to you? If not, it may be time to consider other options that better match your God-given personality, natural strengths and talents, spiritual gifts, and heart's desires. A career counselor or some online self-assessment tests may help provide direction.

Procrastination and the Pursuit of Perfection

Sometimes people are driven by the belief that whatever they do must be done perfectly. This self-imposed pressure can be so psychologically overwhelming that it results in procrastination. If things pile up even higher while a person is procrastinating, their task becomes even more overwhelming, making them want to procrastinate even more. Thus, the desire to accomplish something perfectly can actually result, ironically, in accomplishing nothing!

- Do you feel that you must do things perfectly? If so, give serious thought to how much extra time and energy it takes to move something from "good enough" to the perfection you envision. Is attaining perfection worth the time and energy it will cost you and perhaps others? Think also about your focus. Is it on your performance more than the purpose and potential impact of what you're doing? Experts suggest that focusing on the impact of your task may free you from the pressure of perfectionism and motivate you to roll up your sleeves and get started. From a practical standpoint, most of the time "good enough" really is good enough!

Procrastination and Parkinson's Law

While we are still on the personal journey of self-discovery, we are not yet sure how the puzzle pieces of life fit together. If we are still exploring our natural talents and spiritual gifts, pondering what we're designed by God to do, we may not have discovered our "why"—the motivating purpose that defines and drives our choices. In some circumstances, that lack of directional clarity may cause us to procrastinate, unintentionally fulfilling what is known as Parkinson's Law. Parkinson's Law is the somewhat tongue-in-cheek observation that work expands to fill all the time allotted for its completion. This can play out in two different ways any time we are given a due date or must meet a deadline.

First, consider Parkinson's Law in the context of submitting applications for programs with due dates, such as college admissions, scholarships, job internships, or study abroad programs. When a due date is announced three months in advance, one person, certain about their direction in life, applies immediately. Another person, uncertain about their direction, waits, thinking there is plenty of time to weigh the pros and cons of the opportunity and to think about what they might say on the application. Because the deadline seems a long way off, they don't feel any pressure to decide. Then, at the very last minute, they decide to apply. They scramble to hastily pull their application together and submit it in time to beat the deadline. By procrastinating until the last minute, they fulfill Parkinson's Law: *the work of applying is expanded to fill all the time allotted for completion.*

Now, consider Parkinson's Law in the context of workplace projects. Some people fulfill Parkinson's Law in the way just described: with a mad last-minute scramble to complete a project by its due date. Others finish a project quickly, well ahead of the due date, but continue to add detail after detail, daily tweaking the project right up to the due date. They, too, fulfill Parkinson's Law: *through continual tweaks and additions, the work is expanded to fill all the time allotted for completion.*

There is no time frame for the journey of self-discovery. It takes time, sometimes a great deal of time, to fully explore your inborn personality, natural talents, and spiritual gifts—and there is no "deadline." During this long period, you may need to make important decisions related to your life direction, such as the one in the previous application example.

As that example illustrates, we sometimes procrastinate because we're just not sure about what decision to make. But when we're making potentially life-altering decisions, procrastination is actually a good thing! A time of thoughtful hesitation allows us to wait for God's direction. In fact, we shouldn't even think of this as procrastination; we should reframe it as a time of waiting on God.

- Whenever you thoughtfully and prayerfully wait on God, you're doing exactly what Proverbs 4:26 instructs us to do: "Give careful thought to the paths for your feet." Here are some other verses you may want to meditate on when you are contemplating important decisions:

Show me the way I should go,
for to you I entrust my life.

PSALM 143:8

No eye has seen any God besides you,
who acts on behalf of those who wait for him.

ISAIAH 64:4

Be still in the presence of the Lord,
and wait patiently for him to act.

PSALM 37:7 NLT

Your word is a lamp for my feet,
a light on my path.

PSALM 119:105

"I know the plans I have for you,"
declares the Lord, "plans to prosper you
and not to harm you, plans to give you
hope and a future."

JEREMIAH 29:11

How to Interrupt Overwhelm

Imagine a day when your thinking is fuzzy and you can't focus. Your chest feels tight. Anxiety is mounting and you're almost ready to cry. There is too much on your plate, and you have no idea how you will ever get it all done. You're overwhelmed. Now what?

When we find ourselves fragile, frayed, and overwhelmed, there are several ways to interrupt our panic and restore ourselves to peace. You can use these short-term "rescue" measures to comfort yourself, regain a sense of balance, and get back on track.

Try one, several, or all of the following ideas, and not necessarily in the order they are listed. However, if possible, do each of them at least once so that you can discover which ones are most helpful to you. Any one of them will help you move back toward calm and productivity. It may be most helpful to do several.

Breathe Differently

This quick and very simple way to breathe a little differently will help suppress the fight-or-flight response that kicks in when you feel overwhelmed:

> Breathe in deeply as you count to four, making your belly expand as your lungs fill with air.

Exhale slowly as you count to eight, so that breathing out takes twice as long as breathing in. Do this several times.

When you breathe this way, the diaphragm moves, stimulating the calming function of the vagus nerve. This will slow your heart rate, lower your blood pressure, and help you feel more calm.

Use All Five Senses

This 5-4-3-2-1 technique will ground you in the present moment and allow your senses to briefly distract you from the thoughts that are overwhelming you.[50]

5: See

Scan your environment and name five things that you see.

4: Hear

Listen until you can name four things that you hear.

3: Touch

Touch three things around you, such as the chair you're sitting in, or the pages of this book or the device you're reading it on.

2: Smell

Breathe in through your nose and identify two things that you smell.

1: Taste

Name one thing you taste, such as your coffee or water, gum, lip balm, or even just the inside of your mouth.

Step Away

Physically move away from whatever is feeding your feeling of being overwhelmed—maybe a pile of papers on your desk, a mess in your kitchen, a puddle your dog left on the floor, or a difficult conversation. If possible, go outside and take a brief walk, or at least breathe some fresh air for a few minutes. Even a short break in a different physical space can help to renew your perspective.

Order Your Environment

If your desk or immediate environment is cluttered, it can add to your sense of being overwhelmed. Experts suggest that by just organizing your desk or some aspect of your near surroundings, you can ease a little bit of your brain's burden. They're not talking about a major deep cleaning, just bringing a little order to your immediate physical space by stacking papers, dusting, or organizing the pens and paper clips on your desk.

Answer This One Question

An article that appeared in the *Harvard Business Review* suggests, "Ask yourself the question, 'What one or two things, if taken off my plate would alleviate 80% of the stress I feel right now?'"[51] This is a great question to consider, even if it's not actually possible to take those one or two things off your plate. It's helpful just to identify the main reason you feel so overwhelmed. If you can find extra support for yourself as you deal with this thing that burdens you most, or if you can delegate any part of it, by all means do so.

Put It On Paper

When we try to remember everything we need to do, or rely on sticky notes, it's hard not to feel overwhelmed. Getting it all out of our head and onto paper allows us to take an objective look at everything. Putting our to-do's in writing allows us to begin to organize them in ways that will bring order to our chaos. Start with a brain dump: write a master list of every single thing you must do, even little chores like buying stamps.

MASTER LIST
- Buy stamps
- Call Mom
- Sign birthday card
- RSVP to wedding invitation
- Do laundry
- Mow lawn

Next, organize your tasks. On a separate sheet of paper, make three headings:

1. Do Now

2. Do Later

3. Delegate or Decline

Assign every item on your master list to one of these three categories. Then, within each category, number the tasks in order of their priority, and/or "chunk" the tasks into groups of similar things that could be done in the same time period. For example, you could group all of the phone calls you need to make. You could also group small tasks that can each be done very quickly: sign a birthday card, click to accept or decline attendance at a meeting, or RSVP online to a wedding invitation.

DO NOW
 1. Sign birthday card
 2. RSVP to wedding invitation

DO LATER
 1. Do laundry
 2. Call Mom

DELEGATE / DECLINE
 1. Mow lawn
 2. Buy stamps

This grouping and acting on small tasks is a time-management strategy called the "two-minute rule."[52] The idea is that if a task takes less than two minutes to complete, do it now. Grouping all your quick tasks together just makes sense; it gets a lot of little things off your plate very fast. Alternatively, if all of your to-do's are of equal priority and/or "chunkable," group like with like and don't bother making the three lists. Tackle the chunks that require the most energy during the time of day when you are at your best.

Cast Your Cares

As mentioned at the close of chapter one, more than anyone else you will ever meet, Jesus understands what it is to feel overwhelmed. He has felt what you're feeling and more. The Bible tells us, "Cast all your cares on him. For he cares for you" (1 Peter 5:7 RGT). You can talk to him about all that's overwhelming you. He truly understands, and as the verse says, he cares for *you* personally.

O God, listen to my cry! Hear my prayer! From the ends of the earth, I cry to you for help when my heart is overwhelmed. Lead me to the towering rock of safety, for you are my safe refuge, a fortress where my enemies cannot reach me.

PSALM 61:1-3 NLT

Talk to Yourself

We all have a running inner dialogue with ourselves. Our self-talk can either be negative or positive. Unfortunately, according to research, we tend to speak more negatively than positively to ourselves, and often less kindly than we would speak to a friend or loved one. Negative, critical self-talk is never helpful, but it's especially unhelpful when we're feeling overwhelmed. But we can change that! One counselor suggests that we encourage ourselves with self-talk about our progress and successes, such as:[53]

- "That wasn't perfect, but I handled that situation better than I normally do."

- "It was a tough situation, but I managed to keep my temper. Yay!"

- "Even though my project isn't finished, I definitely made progress today."

It's also helpful to swap out certain words that may have crept into our self-talk. Instead of telling yourself, "I *have to* ..." say, more optimistically, "I *get to*..." Instead of scolding yourself with the word *should* ("I *should* have accomplished more today"), swap it for *prefer*: "I would *prefer* to have accomplished more." These are subtle changes, but they are more self-affirming.

Build a Fence for the Future

"First aid" measures, such as the ones just described, help to temporarily rescue us when we're overwhelmed. What's most needed for the future, however, are strategies to keep ourselves from becoming overwhelmed time and time again. While it's hard to think about the future when we're up to our eyeballs in the present, we must. If we want our future to be less overwhelming than our present, we can't stay so busy chasing cats that we never stop to build a fence to corral the cats!

To build a strong overwhelm-prevention fence, we need three things: monotasking tools, a few tips and tricks to help us overwhelm-proof our lives, and a surprising Secret Weapon. Let's take a closer look at each of these.

1. Monotasking Tools

Since we now know that the brain works best when we focus on just one thing at a time, we have a reason to fight the urge to multitask. There are several time management strategies that can help us monotask at home and at work. Here is a quick look at some of the most popular:

Pomodoro Technique

This technique consists of 25-minute sessions of focused work, followed by 5-minute breaks. After four work/break cycles, there is a longer 15–30 minute break. During the breaks the goal is to do something that's not mentally taxing, such as stretching or listening to music so that the brain gets a break. To use the Pomodoro method, you  need a timer. You can download a Pomodoro app to your phone, or use a timer specifically programmed for Pomodoro, or simply use a kitchen timer.

Benefits: The Pomodoro method helps break the multitasking habit by enabling users to focus on just one thing. Thus, the method improves the ability to focus, and the built-in breaks decrease brain fatigue.

Fun fact: Pomodoro was developed by a university student who was struggling to manage his time. He developed this method using a kitchen timer that was shaped like a tomato. *Pomodoro* is the Italian word for *tomato*.

Personal impression: I downloaded a Pomodoro app to my phone and used it while writing this chapter. It was helpful. I like it. It's like interval training for the brain.

Time Blocking

The time blocking method can help people make the utmost of their time. With time blocking, users create visual blocks of time on a calendar and designate specific blocks for all the different tasks they want to do throughout the day. Similar tasks are batched together, and each batch is assigned to a time block. Every block of time on the calendar contains a single task or a batch of similar tasks. Users fill their entire daily schedule with time blocks for everything from tending to email and working on projects to scheduling breaks, exercise, and family time.

Benefits: Like the Pomodoro method, time blocking helps break the multitasking habit by helping users focus on one thing at a time. Time blocking also helps users prioritize their tasks, resist the urge to procrastinate, and regain a sense of control over their time.

Other Monotasking Tools

The Resources section at the back of this book includes links to information about two other ways to monotask when managing time: the GTD (Getting Things Done) method and Timeboxing. A third method, the two-minute rule, was explained previously.

2. Tips and Tricks

Everyone has the same twenty-four hours of time in their day, but people use those hours in vastly different ways. How we use our time can mean the difference between being on top of the pile or lying underneath it, overwhelmed. Here are some tips and tricks from the experts.

Power Naps

What do Stephen King and entrepreneur Mark Cuban have in common with historical figures like Albert Einstein, Leonardo da Vinci, and John F. Kennedy? Naps! Throughout history, some of the most famous, creative, and highly accomplished people have been "power nappers."[54]

A 20–30 minute power nap gives a boost to memory, alertness, and mood while also reducing stress. Napping also has a positive effect on cognitive functions, such as the ability to complete complex tasks. Thus, power napping can play an important role in helping to "overwhelm-proof" your life.

Most Important Tasks (MITs)

Great time managers start each day by identifying their MITs—Most Important Tasks. MITs are the three to five things they will focus on and try to accomplish first. That way, no matter what else does or doesn't get done, at the end of the day, at least the most important things will have been completed.

As you no doubt know from personal experience, there is no shortage of potential interruptions that can hijack your plan for the day. Our constant challenge is to distinguish between what's *important* and what's *urgent*—and respond accordingly.

Even when something is truly urgent, it doesn't always require instant attention. If we've set aside a time block to work on our MITs, maybe we can address an urgent matter when our block of focus-time is over. If an urgent matter is more important than the MIT we're in the middle of, we may choose to act on it right then. The point is that our MITs don't always have to succumb to the tyranny of the urgent.

Organization

The queen of organization, Martha Stewart, has said, "Life is too complicated not to be orderly."[55] One expression of her passion for order is her very comprehensive book about organizing just about every aspect of life (*Martha Stewart's Organizing: The Manual for Bringing Order to Your Life, Home, and Routines*). In that book, she explains that getting organized "will save you so much time in the long run ... and leave you free to spend less time on chores [and] more time for the activities that prove meaningful to you."[56] Her words underscore the fact that disorganization robs us of time and helps pave the way to feeling overwhelmed.

If you have a lot of organizing to do, don't let the enormity of that task overwhelm you! Pick one area at a time to focus on (monotasking), such as one cluttered closet. Go project by project as you are able, and don't worry about how long it may take you to get completely organized. Little by little, you will get there, recouping more time and peace of mind with each completed project.

3. The Secret Weapon: "Wasting" Time

How many times have you heard someone say, "My best ideas come to me when I'm in the shower"?

The same thing sometimes happens when people are driving long distances or out walking or running. When our thoughts are free to roam, our unconscious mind goes into creative mode, often surprising us with solutions to problems and new ideas about all kinds of things.

Psychologist and author Alice Boyes says, "When I go for a walk … I let my mind drift without directing it too much…. Solutions to problems magically emerge, and what I should prioritize becomes clearer without effort." She explains that when we feel overwhelmed, instead of procrastinating by tuning in to a podcast or a TV show, it might be more beneficial to just let our thoughts freely roam. When we distract ourselves with entertainment, we may be missing out on the "productivity potential" of our drifting minds.[57]

"Our brains really benefit when we 'waste time,'" says Dr. Christine Carter. "When we let ourselves daydream or our minds wander, an area of our brain comes online that is responsible for creative insight, and our best work comes from those creative insights."[58] Ultimately, the very best overwhelm-prevention strategy of all may be to simply allow ourselves the luxury of "wasting" some time.

Afterword

12 Questions to Think About

As we have seen, in today's "too much" world, it's very easy to get overwhelmed. When we must function in ways that conflict with how we're wired, it makes us even more vulnerable to being overwhelmed.

But if we can live in ways that are compatible with our natural personalities, strengths and talents, spiritual gifts, and heart's desires, we are more insulated from many of the things that might otherwise overwhelm us.

To make wise decisions that help protect us from being overwhelmed, we need keen self-awareness and a strong grip on what matters most and why. The questions below can help clarify your thinking about 12 vital aspects of your life.

Priorities

1. Who or what has first place in your life?

2. After that, what are your highest priorities?

People

3. Who are your "priority people," the individuals you feel closest to and most want to spend your time with?

Self

4. Is your own physical, mental, and spiritual well-being one of your priorities?

5. Do you allow yourself to "waste time" by daydreaming and letting your thoughts drift freely?

Stuff

6. How much of your time do you want to spend organizing, maintaining, and caring for material possessions?

Natural Strengths and Talents

7. What are your natural, inborn strengths and talents?

8. If you did not have the opportunity to nurture and develop your natural strengths and talents when you were a child, how might you do that now?

9. Do your work and activities allow you to use your strengths and talents in ways that are fulfilling to you?

Spiritual Gifts

10. If you are a Christ follower,[59] have you identified your spiritual gifts? If not, consider taking one of the surveys listed in the Resources section.

11. If you aren't using your spiritual gifts at this point in your life, what do you feel drawn to do that would make use of them?

Purpose

12. Based on your answers to the previous questions, how would you answer this final one: What were you born to do?

Resources

Personality and Strengths

Personality, Career, IQ, and Relationships Self-Tests

- psychologytoday.com/us/tests

Introvert, Extrovert, or Ambivert Quiz

- quiz.scienceofpeople.com/ambivert

Marcus Buckingham and Donald O. Clifton, *Now Discover Your Strengths: The Revolutionary Gallup Program That Shows You How to Develop Your Unique Talents and Strengths*, 20th anniversary ed. (Washington, DC: Gallup Press, 2020)

Spiritual Gifts

Team Ministry Spiritual Gifts Survey (free online)

- gifts.churchgrowth.org/spiritual-gifts-survey

Individual Spiritual Gifts Discovery Tool (free online)

- Click "Spiritual Gifts Survey" on this page: lifeway.com/en/articles/women-leadership-spiritual-gifts-growth-service

C. Pete Wagner, *Finding Your Spiritual Gifts: The Easy to Use, Self-Guided Questionnaire*, updated and expanded ed. (Minneapolis: Chosen Books, 2017)

Priorities and Monotasking

Charles E. Hummel, *Tyranny of the Urgent, revised and expanded ed.* (Downers Grove, IL: InterVarsity Press, 2013)

Gain Focus and Productivity with the Pomodoro Technique

- asana.com/resources/pomodoro-technique

Time Blocking and Timeboxing

- Scan the QR code to learn more about the differences between time blocking and timeboxing.

- timedoctor.com/blog/time-blocking

- asana.com/resources/what-is-time-blocking

- timedoctor.com/blog/timeboxing

GTD (Getting Things Done)

- gettingthingsdone.com/what-is-gtd

- *Getting Things Done: The Art of Stress-Free Productivity, updated ed.* (New York: Penguin, 2015)

Videos

Lecture: Christine Carter, PhD, "Full Plate, Empty Life: How to Achieve More by Doing Less," youtube.com/watch?v=5TLHKTciPaM

Music: "Big Daddy Weave—Overwhelmed Live," youtube.com/watch?v=XD0nzqLdYuo

Just for fun: "Cat Herders" (Super Bowl commercial, January 2000), youtube.com/watch?v=m _MaJDK3VNE

Acknowledgments

I am grateful for the many friends, too numerous to list, who encouraged me and prayed for me as this book was being written. Thank you all!

I especially want to thank my son, Chris, for his careful reading of the final manuscript. Chris, because of your thoughtful insights and many good suggestions, this is a much better book than it would otherwise have been! Thank you so much. You're the best!

Notes

1   Megan Dalla-Camina, "How to Deal with Overwhelm," April 26, 2023. *Psychology Today: https://www .psychologytoday.com/us/blog/real-women/202303/how -to-deal-with-overwhelm.*

2   Christopher Schimming, MD, "Cognitive Overload: When Processing Information Becomes a Problem," March 18, 2022. *Mayo Clinic: https://www.mayoclinichealthsystem .org/hometown-health/speaking-of-health/cognitive -overload.*

3   The Decision Lab, "Information Overload." *https://thedecisionlab.com/reference-guide/psychology /information-overload.*

4   Libby Simon, "How Information Overload Affects the Brain," March 25, 2018. *PsychCentral: https://pyschcentral .com/pro/how-information-overload-affects-the-brain#1.*

5   Estimated values taken from the following sources: Aditya Rayaprolu, "How Much Data Is Created Evey Day in 2024?" March 12, 2024, *TechJury: https://techjury .net/blog/how-much-data-is-created-every-day/*; Simon Kemp, "5 Billion Social Media Users," January 31, 2024, *Datareportal: https://datareportal.com/reports/digital -2024-deep-dive-5-billion-social-media-users#:~:text =There%205.04%20billion%20social,new%20 users%20every%20single%20second*; Jimit Bagadiya, "38 Facebook Statistics and Facts for Every Marketer in 2024," February 22, 2024, *SocialPilot: https://www .socialpilot.co/facebook-marketing/facebook-statistics #:~:text=On%20average%2C%20350%20million%20 photos,by%20Facebook%20users%20each%20day*; Mary Lister, "31 Mind-Boggling Instagram Stats & Facts for 2024," January 14, 2024, *WordStream: https://www .wordstream.com/blog/ws/2017/04/20/instagram-statistics*;

Adam Hayes, "YouTube Stats: Everything You Need to Know in 2024!" February 20, 2024, *Wyzolw: https:// www.wyzowl.com/youtube-stats/.*

6   Kevin Bartley, "Big Data Statistics: How Much Data Is There in the World?" August 27, 2023. *Rivery: https:// rivery.io/blog/big-data-statistics-how-much-data-is-there -in-the-world/#:~:text=90%25%20percent%20of%20 the%20world's,the%20world%20doubles%20in%20size.*

7   Joshua Becker, "About Becoming Minimalist." *https://www .becomingminimalist.com/becoming-minimalist-start-here/.*

8   Joshua Becker, Facebook page, "becoming minimalist." *https://www.facebook.com/becomingminimalist.*

9   Jim Stone, "Overwhelmed Much?" November 16, 2015. *Psychology Today: https://www.psychologytoday .com/us/blog/clear-organized-and-motivated/201511 /overwhelmed-much.*

10 Colleen McClain et al., "How Americans View Data Privacy," October 18, 2023. *Pew Research Center: https://www.pewresearch.org/internet/2023/10/18/how -americans-view-data-privacy/.*

11 Stone, "Overwhelmed Much?"

12 Ashley Olivine, "Signs of Being Overwhelmed: What Helps?" September 14, 2023. *Verywell Health: https://www.verywellhealth.com/overwhelmed-7693323.*

13 Christine Carter, "Full Plate, Empty Life: How to Achieve More by Doing Less," posted April 1, 2015. *YouTube: https://www.youtube.com/watch?v=5TLHKTciPaM&list =PLeCh1VER8s5xCagwAtyz4tx-sGf6GYvTo&index=5.*

14 Summary of article by Rebecca Zucker, "How to Deal with Constantly Feeling Overwhelmed," October 10, 2019. *Harvard Business Review: https://hbr.org/2019/10 /how-to-deal-with-constantly-feeling-overwhelmed.*

15 Alice Boyes, "5 Mistakes We Make When We're Overwhelmed," April 27, 2001. *Harvard Business Review*: *https://hbr.org/2021/04/5-mistakes-we-make-when-were-overwhelmed?ab=at_art_art_1x4_s03*.

16 Olivine, "Signs of Being Overwhelmed"; Sanjana Gupta, "What Does It Mean to Feel Overwhelmed?" *https://verywellmind.com/feeling-overwhelmed-symptoms-causes-and-coping-5425548*.

17 Charles Stanley, *Life Principles Bible*, note on Psalm 117:2, p. 703.

18 Dr. David Jeremiah, *Forward: Discovering God's Presence and Purpose in Your Tomorrow* (Nashville: Thomas Nelson, 2020), 36.

19 "The Westminster Shorter Catechism." *The Presbytery of the United States: https://www.westminsterconfession.org/resources/confessional-standards/the-westminster-shorter-catechism*.

20 Barbara Reich, *Secrets of an Organized Mom: From the Overflowing Closets to the Chaotic Play Areas: A Room-By-Room Guide to Decluttering and Streamlining Your Home for a Happier Family* (New York: Atria Books, 2013), 191.

21 J. Vaughan, "Prepared Works," Ephesians 2:10. *Bible Hub: https://biblehub.com/sermons/auth/vaughan/prepared_works.htm*.

22 Henry Alford, *Greek Testament Critical Exegetical Commentary, Ephesians 2. Bible Hub: https://biblehub.com/commentaries/alford/ephesians/2*.

23 Kristeen Cherney, "Why Twins Don't Have Identical Fingerprints," May 30, 3023. *Healthline: https://www.healthline.com/health/do-identical-twins-have-the-same-fingerprints*."

24 See Marcus Buckingham and Donald O. Clifton, *Now, Discover Your Strengths* (New York: The Free Press, 2001), 31, 67–75.

25 *Matthew Henry's Commentary*, Psalm 37, verses 1–6. *Bible Gateway: https://www.biblegateway.com/resources /matthew-henry/Ps.37.1-Ps.37.6.*

26 Carter, "Full Plate, Empty Life."

27 Jeremiah, *Forward*.

28 Charles E. Hummel, *Tyranny of the Urgent*, revised and expanded ed. (Downers Grove, IL: InterVarsity Press, 2013), 17 (Kindle).

29 Sheon Han, "You Can Only Maintain So Many Close Relationships," May 20, 2021. *The Atlantic: https://www .theatlantic.com/family/archive/2021/05/robin-dunbar -explains-circles-friendship-dunbars-number/618931.*

30 Doug Bender, "Why Self Care Is NOT Selfish," August 18, 2022. *I Am Second: https://blog.iamsecond.com/why-self -care-is-not-selfish.*

31 Bender, "Why Self Care Is NOT Selfish."

32 Scott Monty, "The Barrenness of a Busy Life," blog, July 30, 2018, *https://www.scottmonty.com/.* See also his X post, @ScottMonty, February 23, 2020, *https://twitter .com/ScottMonty/status/1231782232815284224.*

33 Hummel, *Tyranny of the Urgent*, loc. 50 of 265, Kindle.

34 Hummel, *Tyranny of the Urgent*, loc. 214, Kindle.

35 Reich, *Secrets of an Organized Mom*, 188.

36 Hummel, *Tyranny of the Urgent*, loc. 169, Kindle.

37 "Why Are Cats So Independent?" *PetPlace: https://www .petplace.com/article/cats/pet-behavior-training/why-are -cats-so-independent.*

38 Kevin P. Madore and Anthony D. Wagner, "Multicosts of Multitasking," *Cerebrum* (March/April 2019). *National Library of Medicine: https://www.ncbi.nlm.nih.gov/pmc /articles/PMC7075496/pdf/cer-04-19.pdf.*

39 Madore and Wagner, "Multicosts of Multitasking."

40 Dana Foundation, "How We Learn." *https://dana.org /resource/how-we-learn/.*

41 Lesley University, "Why Brain Overload Happens." *https://lesley.edu/article/why-brain-overload-happens.*

42 Jade Wu, "8 Strategies to Manage Overwhelming Feelings," May 20, 2020. *Psychology Today: https://www.psychologytoday.com/us/blog/the-savvy -psychologist/202005/8-strategies-to-manage -overwhelming-feelings.*

43 "Why Multitasking Doesn't Work," March 9, 2021. *Cleveland Clinic: https://health.clevelandclinic.org/science -clear-multitasking-doesnt-work.*

44 Julia Martins, "Multitasking Doesn't Work—Here's What Does," February 12, 2024. *Asana: https://asana.com /resources/multitasking.*

45 Carter, "Full Plate, Empty Life."

46 Martins, "Multitasking Doesn't Work."

47 Garth Sundem, "This Is Your Brain on Multitasking," February 24, 2012. *Psychology Today: https://www .psychologytoday.com/us/blog/brain-trust/201202/is-your -brain-multitasking.*

48 Wu, "8 Strategies to Manage Overwhelming Feelings."

49 Julia Martins, "The Secret to Stop Procrastinating at Work," February 5, 2024. *Asana: https://asana.com /resources/tips-stop-procrastinating.*

50 Wu, "8 Strategies to Manage Overwhelming Feelings."

51   Zucker, "How to Deal with Constantly Feeling Overwhelmed."

52   The "two-minute rule" was coined by David Allen in his book *Getting Things Done: The Art of Stress-Free Productivity* (New York: Penguin, 2001), 131.

53   Meg Selig, "8 Self-Talk Solutions That Can Ease Mental Stress," October 23, 2023. *Psychology Today: https://www.psychologytoday.com/us/blog/changepower /202310/8-self-talk-solutions-that-can-ease-mental-stress.*

54   Restworks, "22 Famous Nappers: How Napping Was These People's Key to Success." *https://rest.works/en /article/famous-nappers-in-history/.*

55   John Rampton, "101 Powerful Productivity Quotes That Will Inspire You to Work Harder, Smarter," March 13, 2019. *Calendar Productivity Center: https://www .calendar.com/blog/101-powerful-productivity-quotes -that-will-inspire-you-to-work-harder-smarter/.*

56   *Martha Stewart's Organizing: The Manual for Bringing Order to Your Life, Home, and Routines* (Boston: Houghton Mifflin Harcourt, 2020), 6.

57   Boyes, "5 Mistakes We Make When We're Overwhelmed."

58   Carter, "Full Plate, Empty Life."

59   If you are not a Christ follower but are interested in knowing more, this website may be helpful: *https://www .cru.org/us/en/how-to-know-god.html.*

Other Bible translations used:

About the Author

Debbie Barr is an author, health educator, and speaker with a passion for encouraging people to engage deeply with God as they journey through tough times.

She earned her bachelor's degree in journalism from the Pennsylvania State University and her master's degree in health education from East Carolina University. A master certified health education specialist (MCHES®), Debbie is especially interested in health and wellness, health literacy, and Christian growth.

She lives in Bermuda Run, North Carolina.

You can learn more about Debbie by visiting her website (debbiebarr.com), her Amazon author page (amazon.com/author/debbiebarr) or her Linkedin profile (www.linkedin.com/in/debbiebarr).

Hope and Healing

Unmasking Emotional Abuse

Six Steps to Reduce Stress

Ten Tips for Parenting the Smartphone Generation

Five Keys to Dealing with Depression

Seven Answers for Anxiety

Five Keys to Raising Boys

Freedom From Shame

Five Keys to Health and Healing

When a Loved One Is Addicted

Social Media and Depression

Rebuilding Trust after Betrayal

How to Deal with Toxic People

The Power of Connection

Why Failure Is Never Final

Find Your Purpose in Life

Here Today, Ghosted Tomorrow

Caregiving

Forgiveness

The Mystery of Waiting

Overwhelmed